DAVID GILMOUR

A LIFE IN MUSIC

<u>WRITTEN BY:</u>
DUNFREY CANEMAN

David Gilmour

© <u>Dunfrey Caneman, 2024</u>.

<u>DISCLAIMER</u>

<u>For additional information and reviews, please contact</u>:

Dunfrey Caneman on the Amazon webpage.

his services to music. His guitar playing has consistently ranked among the greatest of all time, with Rolling Stone magazine placing him at number 28 on their prestigious list.

Beyond music, Gilmour has used his platform to champion various social and political causes. A staunch advocate for environmental protection, animal rights, and humanitarian aid, he has donated millions of pounds to charities and organisations dedicated to making a positive impact on the world.In his personal life, Gilmour has found love and partnership with novelist Polly Samson. Their collaborative songwriting efforts have yielded some of his most poignant and evocative lyrics, adding a new dimension to his artistic expression.

Gilmour's journey is an attestation to the transformative power of music. His contributions to Pink Floyd and his solo career have left an enduring mark on the rock and roll landscape. But beyond his musical achievements, his strong dedication to social justice and his enduring legacy as a humanitarian speak volumes about his character and values.

musicians, some students, some seasonal performers, converged to form Jokers Wild. Their story is one of ambition, experimentation, and pursuing a musical identity in a rapidly evolving landscape.

It was late 1963 when Dave Altham, a piano and saxophone player studying at Trinity College, joined forces with Tony Sainty, a former choirboy turned bassist, along with Johnny Gordon and Clive Welham, both experienced musicians from the Ramblers. Completing the lineup was a young guitarist named David Gilmour, whose talent would later propel him to international fame with Pink Floyd.

Unlike many bands of the era, Jokers Wild embraced vocal harmonies, inspired by the Beatles and the Hollies. They weren't afraid to tackle complex arrangements, even covering intricate Beach Boys and Four Seasons songs. Their versatility earned them gigs at youth clubs, village halls, and prestigious venues like the Dorothy, Guildhall, and Victoria, where they held a

EARLY YEARS

David Jon Gilmour's formative years were steeped in the vibrant cultural milieu of post-war Cambridge, England. Born on March 6, 1946, into an academic family, his father, Douglas Gilmour, was a respected senior lecturer in zoology at the University of Cambridge, while his mother, Sylvia, was a trained teacher who later transitioned to a career as a film editor for the BBC. His childhood was marked by a series of relocations within Cambridge, eventually settling in the idyllic village of Grantchester. The picturesque meadows and tranquil setting would later serve as inspiration for some of Pink Floyd's most evocative lyrics.

From a young age, Gilmour's parents nurtured his budding interest in music. In 1954, he acquired his first single, Bill Haley's "Rock Around the Clock," a pivotal moment that ignited his passion for rock and roll. The following year, Elvis Presley's "Heartbreak Hotel" further fueled his musical fire, while the Everly Brothers' "Bye Bye Love" sparked a specific interest in the guitar. A self-taught musician, Gilmour's initial foray into guitar playing involved borrowing (and never returning) an

prove useful in his later travels. During his time at the college, Gilmour reconnected with Barrett, who was also a student there. The two spent countless hours practising guitar together, jamming in the college's lunchroom and nurturing their shared musical aspirations. This period of intense collaboration laid the groundwork for their future partnership in Pink Floyd.

Gilmour joined the blues rock band Jokers Wild, a group that included future Pink Floyd drummer Nick Mason. The band recorded a one-sided album and a single, but their limited release ensured they remained a local phenomenon.

Amidst the frenzy of 1960s Cambridge, a group of young

residency at Les Jeux Interdits, a popular haunt for foreign language students. The band's ambitions extended beyond local gigs. They played college balls, travelled to London for performances, and even shared the stage with the legendary Animals. Their youthful energy and eclectic repertoire attracted a growing fanbase.

A pivotal moment occurred in October 1965, when Jokers Wild performed at the 21st birthday party of Rose and Libby January. The event was a convergence of musical talent, with Paul Simon, then touring the UK, joining the band for an impromptu rendition of "Johnny B. Goode." Notably, Pink Floyd, the band Gilmour would later join, was also present. This gathering, immortalised in a photograph, foreshadowed the interconnectedness of the British music scene. Buoyed by their growing popularity, Jokers Wild recorded five tracks at Regent Sound Studio in London's Tin Pan Alley. These recordings, intended for their fans, captured the essence of their early sound. As the band matured, so did their musical tastes. With the departure of Sainty and the arrival of David's brother, Peter Gilmour, on bass, Jokers Wild began incorporating soul, R&B, and Motown influences into their sets. This shift opened doors to new opportunities, including gigs at US Air Force bases.

David Gilmour

Gilmour's restless spirit and thirst for adventure led him to hitchhike to Saint-Tropez, France, in 1965. There, he reunited with Barrett and a group of friends who had driven down from England. Their time in France was marked by both musical exploration and run-ins with the law, including an arrest for busking. Undeterred, Gilmour and Barrett continued their travels, venturing to Paris, where they camped outside the city and immersed themselves in the cultural riches of the Louvre. To support himself during this period, Gilmour took on various odd jobs, most notably as the driver and assistant for the renowned fashion designer Ossie Clark.

In 1966, Jokers Wild aimed for professional success. They sought guidance from industry figures, including Brian Somerville, the Beatles' publicity manager, and Jonathan King, a fellow student of Altham's. King produced their next single, a cover of Sam and Dave's "You Don't Know Like I Know," but its release was shelved when the original gained traction. Personnel changes continued as Clive Welham, hampered by a wrist injury, left the band and was replaced by drummer Willie Wilson. The summer of 1966 saw Jokers Wild securing a residency at the Hotel los Monteros in Marbella, Spain. However, Peter Gilmour's departure for university and Johnny Gordon's return to art school led to further lineup changes, with Rick Wills taking over on bass.

David Gilmour

In mid-1967, Gilmour's musical journey took another turn when he travelled to France, first to St. Etienne and then to Paris, with Rick Wills and Willie Wilson, former members of Jokers Wild. The trio performed under the names Flowers and Bullitt, but their efforts met with limited success. Financial hardship and the theft of their equipment forced them to return to England, where their impoverished state was evident as they pushed their empty tour bus off the ferry. Their journey took them as far as St. Tropez, but it was ultimately cut short when David Gilmour became ill in 1967. Jokers Wild's story may have ended there, but its legacy lives on. Gilmour's subsequent success with Pink Floyd cemented his place in rock history. Willie Wilson and Rick Wills went on to play in numerous successful bands, while Johnny Gordon and Peter Gilmour pursued careers in graphic design and accounting, respectively.

Despite these setbacks, Gilmour's determination and musical talent remains undiminished. His experiences in France had broadened his horizons and exposed him to new musical influences. Unbeknownst to him, his path was about to intersect once again with Pink Floyd, setting the stage for a remarkable chapter in the history of rock music.

THE GENESIS OF AN ICON

Gilmour's entry into Pink Floyd marked a pivotal turning point in the band's history. In 1967, the group, comprising his Cambridge schoolmates Syd Barrett, Roger Waters, Nick Mason, and Richard Wright, had released their debut album, "The Piper at the Gates of Dawn." The album's psychedelic soundscapes and Barrett's eccentric songwriting had garnered critical acclaim and a growing cult following. However, behind the scenes, Barrett's mental health was deteriorating rapidly, fueled by his excessive use of LSD and other drugs. During a brief trip to London in May 1967, Gilmour witnessed firsthand the extent of Barrett's decline. He was shocked to find that his friend no longer seemed to recognize him, a stark reminder of the toll that fame and substance abuse had taken on the troubled frontman.

By December 1967, Gilmour had returned to England, and Mason extended an invitation for him to join Pink Floyd. The initial plan was for Gilmour to serve as a stand-in for Barrett during live performances, allowing the band to fulfil their touring commitments while Barrett focused on songwriting. However, the hope that

performances for years to come. The song's hypnotic rhythm, Eastern-inspired melodies, and poetic lyrics, drawn from ancient Chinese texts, create an atmosphere of mystical introspection. It is the only song on the album to feature all five members of Pink Floyd, including Barrett, whose brief guitar solo adds a haunting touch to the track. "Corporal Clegg," another Waters composition, marks a departure from the band's psychedelic roots. It is a satirical anti-war song, featuring a jaunty melody and dark humour. The song's lyrics, filled with ironic references to military life, foreshadow Waters' later exploration of war and its consequences in albums like The Wall and The Final Cut.

The album's title track, "A Saucerful of Secrets," is an ambitious instrumental piece that showcases the band's growing interest in experimental sounds and textures. Inspired by avant-garde composers like Stockhausen, the song featured experimental techniques such as tape loops and musique concrète, chaotic percussion, swirling organs, and dissonant guitar lines, creating a sonic landscape that was both unsettling and captivating. "Jugband Blues," the only song on the album solely written and sung by Barrett, is a poignant farewell to his bandmates and fans. The lyrics, filled with cryptic imagery and introspective musings, reflect

David Gilmour

Barrett's deteriorating mental state and his growing isolation from the world around him.

Several additional songs were recorded during the A Saucerful of Secrets sessions but were ultimately left off the album. These include "Vegetable Man" and "Scream Thy Last Scream," both written by Barrett and intended as a single release. Another Barrett composition, "In the Beechwoods," was also recorded during these sessions. These unreleased tracks, along with other rare recordings, were eventually made available on the compilation album The Early Years 1965-1972, providing a glimpse into the band's creative process during this transitional period.

The album was released in the UK on June 28, 1968, and quickly climbed to number nine on the charts. However, its reception in the United States was less enthusiastic, with the album failing to chart initially. This was partly due to the limited promotional efforts by Tower Records, the band's American label at the time.

Critical response to A Saucerful of Secrets was mixed. Some reviewers praised the album's experimental nature and sonic diversity, while others criticised it for lacking the cohesiveness and songwriting prowess of the band's debut album, The Piper at the Gates of Dawn. In a surprising turn of events, the album finally charted on the Billboard 200 in 2019, peaking at number 158, following a Record Store Day reissue of the mono mix. This belated recognition speaks to the album's enduring appeal and its significance in Pink Floyd's discography.

The album's release history is also noteworthy. The stereo mix was first released on CD in 1988 and was later remastered and reissued in various formats, including the Shine On box set. However, the mono mix, which some fans consider to be the definitive version, remained elusive on CD for many years. It was finally reissued on vinyl for Record Store Day in 2019, leading to the album's unexpected chart debut in the United States.

In retrospect, A Saucerful of Secrets holds a unique place in Pink Floyd's catalogue. It is a transitional album, bridging the gap between the psychedelic experimentation of their early years and the progressive rock epics that would define their later career. Despite its initial mixed reception, the album has grown in stature over time, recognized for its adventurous spirit, diverse soundscapes, and the emotional weight of its songs, particularly "Jugband Blues," Syd Barrett's final contribution to the band. Even Nick Mason, Pink Floyd's drummer, considers A Saucerful of Secrets his favourite album by the band.

David Gilmour

He appreciates its experimental nature and sees it as a significant marker of the band's evolution, stating,

"I think there are ideas contained there that we have continued to use all the way through our career."

*I*n a bold departure from their earlier psychedelic explorations, Pink Floyd unveiled "Ummagumma" in 1969. This double LP, released on EMI's Harvest label, served as a dual sonic portrait of the band at that time. The first disc, a live recording, captured their raw energy and improvisational spirit on stage at Manchester College of Commerce and Mothers club in Birmingham. This live set showcased extended versions of their earlier material, highlighting their evolving mastery of performance dynamics and sonic textures.

The second disc plunged into uncharted territory, offering a glimpse into the individual creative minds of each band member. This experimental suite featured four distinct solo compositions, each reflecting the unique musical vision of Roger Waters, Gilmour, Nick

Mason, and Richard Wright. Waters' "Several Species of Small Furry Animals Gathered Together in a Cave and Grooving with a Pict" was a bizarre soundscape of manipulated vocalisations and tape effects, while Mason's "The Grand Vizier's Garden Party" was a percussive exploration, and Wright's multi-part "Sysyphus" delved into avant-garde electronic textures.

Gilmour, the band's guitarist and vocalist, approached his solo contribution with some apprehension. He later admitted to feeling unsure of his direction and "waffling about, tacking bits and pieces together." The resulting piece, "The Narrow Way," is a three-part suite that encompasses a range of styles, from bluesy guitar riffs to orchestral arrangements. The first part, originally titled "Baby Blue Shuffle in D Major," was performed during a BBC radio session in 1968. The second and third parts, featuring vocal harmonies and a more experimental approach, reveal Gilmour's growing confidence as a songwriter and his willingness to explore new musical territories.

"Ummagumma" was met with generally positive reviews upon its release in November 1969, with critics recognizing the band's adventurous spirit and willingness to push the boundaries of conventional rock music. The album climbed to number five on the UK charts, solidifying Pink Floyd's growing popularity.

Gilmour's musical curiosity extended beyond Pink Floyd. In 1970, he attended the Isle of Wight Festival, where he assisted in the live mix of Jimi Hendrix's performance, a proof of his admiration for the legendary guitarist.

Following the completion of Pink Floyd's work on the "Zabriskie Point" soundtrack in Rome, a project that ended on a somewhat sour note, Pink Floyd returned to London in early 1970 to begin rehearsals for their next album. They brought with them a collection of unused recordings from the Rome sessions, which would serve as the foundation for new material. However, some of these initial ideas, like "The Violent Sequence" (later to become "Us and Them"), would be shelved for future use.

"Atom Heart Mother," released in October 1970, proved to be a more contentious undertaking. The genesis of the album's title track, "Atom Heart Mother," emerged from these early rehearsals. A series of instrumental fragments composed by the band coalesced into a sprawling piece, initially dubbed "Theme from an Imaginary Western" by Gilmour. The earliest documented live performance of this embryonic piece took place on January 17th, 1970, at Hull University. Through these live renditions, the band gradually refined and shaped the structure of the composition. The title track, a sprawling 23-minute composition, was an ambitious collaboration with avant-garde composer Ron Geesin. The piece featured a full orchestra and choir, resulting in a grandiose, sometimes chaotic blend of classical and rock elements.

The recording process was fraught with disagreements and creative clashes, with band members later expressing dissatisfaction with the final product. Waters, in particular, was highly critical of "Atom Heart Mother," famously stating he would rather see it **"thrown into the dustbin and never listened to by anyone ever again."** Gilmour echoed this sentiment, describing the album as **"a load of rubbish"** and suggesting the band was **"scraping the barrel"** creatively at that time.

Gilmour, who at this point had limited songwriting experience, was reportedly instructed by the band to remain at EMI Studios until he had composed a suitable song for the album. The result was "Fat Old Sun," a mellow, folk-infused piece that remains one of Gilmour's personal favourites. This song became a regular fixture in Pink Floyd's live shows during 1970-71 and would later be featured prominently in Gilmour's solo concerts in 2006.

David Gilmour

Despite the internal tensions, "Atom Heart Mother" achieved commercial success, becoming Pink Floyd's first number-one album in the UK. However, it also marked a turning point for the band, as they began to grapple with their artistic direction and creative differences.

Throughout 1970, Pink Floyd embarked on extensive tours of America and Europe, further solidifying their reputation as a live act. However, behind the scenes, the band members were experiencing personal and creative changes that would ultimately shape their future trajectory. Mason and Wright became fathers and settled into domestic life in London, while Gilmour moved to a farmhouse in Essex. Waters, meanwhile, set up a home recording studio, fostering his growing interest in songwriting and production.

Following the mixed reception of "Atom Heart Mother," Pink Floyd embarked on a new creative journey, culminating in the release of "Meddle" in October 1971. This transitional masterpiece marked a turning point for Pink Floyd, showcasing the emergence of Gilmour as a driving creative force within the band. In this album, Gilmour's distinctive guitar work and songwriting prowess began to shape the band's sound, paving the way for their future successes. As a guitarist, he brought a new level of sophistication and expressiveness to the band's sound. His solos on tracks like "One of These Days" and "Echoes" are iconic examples of his melodic sensibility and technical skill.

Beyond his guitar work, Gilmour also emerged as a talented songwriter on "Meddle." He co-wrote "A Pillow of Winds" with Roger Waters, a gentle acoustic ballad that provides a moment of respite amidst the album's more experimental tracks. Gilmour's songwriting shines through in "Fearless," a song he penned himself, which features a distinctive folk-inspired melody and lyrics that touch on themes of courage and perseverance.

Perhaps Gilmour's most significant contribution to "Meddle" is his involvement in the creation of "Echoes," the album's sprawling 23-minute centrepiece. This epic track, which occupies the entire second side of the album, showcases his versatility as a musician and composer. He co-wrote the song with Waters, contributing both music and lyrics. His guitar work on "Echoes" is particularly noteworthy, featuring a wide range of techniques and effects, including the use of a wah-wah pedal in reverse, which creates a distinctive, otherworldly sound. The creation of "Echoes" was a collaborative effort, with all four band members contributing to its development. Gilmour's input was crucial in shaping the song's structure and sound.

David Gilmour

As Pink Floyd continued to evolve and experiment, Gilmour's contributions would become increasingly central to their sound, culminating in the iconic albums of the 1970s and beyond. Just a year later, in June 1972, Pink Floyd released "Obscured by Clouds," the soundtrack to Barbet Schroeder's film "La Vallée." This album showcased a different facet of the band's musical personality, featuring shorter, more concise songs with a noticeable country music influence. The recording process took place at Strawberry Studios in Château d'Hérouville, France, with the band taking two breaks from their Japanese tour to work on the project. "Obscured by Clouds" (1972), while not as widely celebrated as "Meddle," also features notable contributions from Gilmour. He co-wrote "Wot's... Uh the Deal" with Waters, a song that showcases his blues-rock guitar playing and his ability to craft catchy melodies. He also sang lead vocals on several tracks, including "Free Four" and "Childhood's End," the latter of which features lyrics written by him.

Following the experimental ventures of "Meddle" and "Obscured by Clouds," Pink Floyd embarked on a new project that would propel them to unprecedented levels of fame and acclaim: "The Dark Side of the Moon." Recorded between May 1972 and January 1973 at Abbey Road Studios with EMI staff engineer Alan Parsons, this concept album delved into the complexities of human experience, touching upon themes of madness, greed, time, and mortality. Notably, the album's title was a reference to lunacy rather than astronomy, a subtle nod to the psychological depths explored within its tracks.

While Gilmour's contributions to "The Dark Side of the Moon" may not be as overtly prominent as in previous albums, his presence is deeply interwoven into the fabric of the music. As a guitarist, he crafted some of the album's most memorable solos, including the searing, blues-infused lead on "Time" and the delicate, atmospheric textures of "Breathe (In the Air)." Gilmour's distinctive tone and melodic sensibility helped to define the album's sonic landscape, adding a layer of emotional depth and complexity to Waters' lyrics.

Gilmour's influence on "The Dark Side of the Moon" extends beyond his individual contributions to specific tracks. His technical expertise and studio acumen played a crucial role in shaping the album's overall sound. He worked closely with Alan Parsons, experimenting with new recording techniques and technologies to create a sonic landscape that was both innovative and immersive. Gilmour's meticulous attention to detail and his dedication to sonic perfection helped to ensure that every element of the album, from the instrumentation to the sound effects, was carefully crafted to create a cohesive and powerful listening experience.

Following the monumental success of "The Dark Side of the Moon," Pink Floyd entered a period of creative tension and personal turmoil that would ultimately shape their next album, "Wish You Were Here." As they reconvened in the studio in January 1975, the band members found themselves grappling with the weight of their newfound fame and struggling to find a new creative direction. The departure of their trusted engineer, Alan Parsons, who had become successful with his own project, The Alan Parsons Project, added another layer of uncertainty to the process. Gilmour, ever the pragmatic musician, was eager to refine and improve upon the band's existing material. However, the emotional and physical exhaustion from their previous success had left the band members, including Gilmour, feeling creatively drained. Roger Waters, on the other hand, began to envision a new concept that would eventually become the central theme of the album.

The catalyst for this concept came in the form of a simple four-note guitar phrase, composed by Gilmour seemingly by accident. This melancholic melody struck a chord with Waters, reminding him of their former bandmate, Syd Barrett. The songs that emerged from this initial spark served as a poignant reflection on Barrett's rise and fall, exploring themes of absence, alienation, and the ephemeral nature of fame. As the band delved deeper into the creation of "Wish You Were Here," Barrett himself made an unexpected appearance at the studio. His physical transformation was so drastic that the band members initially failed to recognize him. This encounter deeply affected Waters, who was reportedly devastated by the sight of his former friend and collaborator in such a diminished state. The experience further fueled the emotional intensity of the album, adding a layer of personal resonance to the already poignant themes.

In September 1975, "Wish You Were Here" was released to critical acclaim and commercial success, reaching number one on both the UK and US charts. The album's title track, with its haunting refrain and Gilmour's iconic guitar solos, became an instant classic, while the multi-part composition "Shine On You Crazy Diamond" served as a moving tribute to Barrett.

Following the success of "Wish You Were Here," Pink Floyd's internal tensions began to escalate, culminating in the recording of "Animals." Waters, who had become increasingly dominant in the songwriting process, clashed with Gilmour over creative control and the division of royalties. Gilmour, distracted by the birth of his first child, contributed less to the album than he had in the past. Wright, too, found himself marginalised, receiving no songwriting credits on the album for the first time.

Despite these internal conflicts, "Animals" proved to be a commercial success, reaching number two in the UK and number three in the US upon its release in January 1977. The album's Orwellian concept, exploring the themes of social and political control through the allegory of animals, resonated with audiences and critics alike.

However, the accompanying "In the Flesh" tour further exacerbated the tensions within the band. The massive scale of the stadium shows, coupled with Waters' increasingly controlling behaviour, led to a growing sense of alienation and frustration among the other members. By the end of the tour, Gilmour felt a profound sense of disillusionment, believing that the band had achieved everything they had set out to do and that there was nothing left to accomplish together.

In 1975, Gilmour's keen ear for talent led him to discover a young Kate Bush. After receiving a demo tape from a mutual friend, her unique voice and songwriting style captivated him. Recognizing her immense potential, Gilmour took Bush under his wing, financing her first professional recordings and introducing her to industry contacts. This act of generosity and mentorship paved the way for Bush's groundbreaking career, making Gilmour a pivotal figure in the history of British music. Besides his work with Pink Floyd and Kate Bush, Gilmour collaborated with other artists, including folk singer Roy Harper. His guitar work on Harper's 1975 album "HQ" demonstrated his versatility and willingness to explore different musical genres.

Following the monumental success and elaborate staging of "The Wall," Pink Floyd found themselves at a crossroads. Creative tensions, particularly between Roger Waters and Gilmour, had reached a boiling point, leading to a power struggle for control over the band's direction. In the midst of this turmoil, Waters presented two distinct ideas for their next album: a 90-minute demo titled "Bricks in the Wall" and another project that would later become his debut solo album, "The Pros and Cons of Hitch Hiking."

Despite initial reservations from both Mason and Gilmour, the band ultimately chose to pursue the concept of "The Wall." With Bob Ezrin co-producing and contributing a forty-page script, the album's narrative began to take shape. Drawing inspiration from Waters' personal experiences, particularly the loss of his father in World War II, the story centred around Pink, a rock star grappling with isolation, trauma, and the dehumanising effects of fame.

While "The Wall" showcased Waters' songwriting and conceptual vision, Gilmour's contributions were no less significant. As the lead guitarist, he brought his signature sound to the album, infusing its songs with soaring solos and evocative melodies. His guitar work on tracks like "Comfortably Numb," "Young Lust," and "Run Like Hell" became iconic, showcasing his ability to create memorable and emotionally resonant musical moments. Gilmour's influence extended beyond his guitar playing. He co-wrote several songs with Waters, including "Comfortably Numb," which is widely regarded as one of Pink Floyd's greatest achievements. Gilmour's melodic sensibility and lyrical contributions helped to balance Waters' darker and more cynical worldview, adding a layer of emotional complexity to the album.

During the recording of "The Wall," tensions within the band escalated, leading to the dismissal of Richard Wright. This decision further strained the relationship between Waters and Gilmour, who had differing opinions on Wright's contributions. While Waters felt that Wright wasn't pulling his weight, Gilmour believed that Wright's keyboard playing and musical ideas were essential to the band's sound. Despite the internal conflicts, "The Wall" was released in November 1979 to immense commercial success. It topped the charts in the US for 15 weeks and became one of the best-selling albums of all time. The album's success solidified Pink Floyd's status as global superstars, but it also marked a turning point in their career, as the creative tensions that had been simmering beneath the surface began to boil over.

The subsequent tour for "The Wall" was a lavish and ambitious production, featuring elaborate stage sets, giant inflatable puppets, and a full cast of performers. While the tour was a financial success, it further strained the already fragile relationships within the band. Waters, increasingly isolated and controlling, arrived at venues alone and stayed in separate hotels from the rest of the band. Wright, having been fired from the band, was rehired as a salaried musician, becoming the only member to profit from the tour.

The release of "The Final Cut" in 1983 marked the culmination of the creative and personal tensions that had been brewing within Pink Floyd for years. Waters, who had become the dominant creative force in the band, took sole songwriting credit for the album, further alienating Gilmour and Mason. Gilmour's contributions were limited to guitar solos and backing vocals, as Waters asserted complete control over the

David Gilmour

Richard Wright, Gilmour's Pink Floyd bandmate, had recently recorded his own solo album, "Wet Dream."

Gilmour's debut solo album showcased his versatility as a musician and songwriter. While the majority of the tracks embraced a blues-rock aesthetic, showcasing his signature guitar work and soulful vocals, there were also moments of departure. The piano-dominated ballad "So Far Away" revealed a softer, more introspective side of Gilmour, highlighting his ability to craft emotive melodies and heartfelt lyrics. The album's sole single, "There's No Way Out of Here," initially found limited success in Europe but gained traction on album-oriented rock radio stations in the US. Notably, this song was a cover of a track originally recorded by Unicorn, a band Gilmour had previously produced. This choice reflects Gilmour's eclectic taste and his willingness to draw inspiration from diverse sources.

One particularly intriguing aspect of the album's creation is the inclusion of an unused demo that would later evolve into the iconic Pink Floyd song "Comfortably Numb." This early version, co-written with Roger Waters, showcases the collaborative nature of their songwriting process and the genesis of one of their most beloved tracks. Additionally, the song "Short and Sweet," co-written with Roy Harper, exhibits musical elements that foreshadow Pink Floyd's later hit "Run Like Hell."

To promote the album, Gilmour not only engaged in his first-ever interviews with North American media and FM rock radio stations but also produced a five-song promotional film. This film captured a live performance by Gilmour and his band, including his brother Mark on rhythm guitar and Ian McLagan on keyboards, at The Roxy in London. The inclusion of three female backing singers on some tracks added another dimension to the performance, showcasing Gilmour's ability to collaborate and adapt his music to different contexts. Upon its release in May 1978, the album received positive reviews and achieved moderate commercial success. It peaked at number 17 in the UK and number 29 on the Billboard US album charts, eventually earning a Gold certification in the US. Gilmour reflected on the importance of the album for his personal and artistic growth, stating that it was crucial for his "self-respect" and a way to step out from the shadow of Pink Floyd.

Interestingly, some of the music written during the final stages of Gilmour's solo album, but ultimately left unused, found its way into Pink Floyd's magnum opus, "The Wall." The haunting melody and evocative lyrics of "Comfortably Numb," arguably one of the band's most iconic songs, were born out of these solo sessions, a

David Gilmour

Upon its release in March 1984, "About Face" received positive reviews and achieved commercial success, reaching number 21 on the UK Albums Chart and number 32 on the US Billboard Top 200 Albums chart. The singles "Blue Light" and "Love on the Air" were released to further promote the album, with "Blue Light" making a notable impact on the US charts. The album's success was a testament to Gilmour's enduring popularity and his ability to connect with audiences through his music.

In subsequent years, Gilmour would reflect on "About Face" with a mix of pride and introspection. While acknowledging its strengths and "great moments," he also expressed a feeling that the overall sound of the album was somewhat dated, reflecting the production style of the 1980s. Nevertheless, "About Face" remains an important milestone in Gilmour's solo career, showcasing his diverse musical influences, his lyrical depth, and his unwavering commitment to artistic expression. The album's creation and release also coincided with a pivotal moment in Pink Floyd's history. As the band's future hung in the balance, Gilmour's solo project served as a creative outlet and a personal statement. It allowed him to explore his own musical identity outside the context of Pink Floyd, ultimately strengthening his confidence and paving the way for his continued success as both a solo artist and a member of the band.

To promote the album, Gilmour embarked on a European and US tour, supported by the quirky post-punk band The Television Personalities. However, the tour was not without its challenges. The Television Personalities were abruptly dropped from the lineup after their singer, Dan Treacy, revealed the address of former Pink Floyd frontman Syd Barrett on stage, a breach of privacy that Gilmour found unacceptable. Despite some setbacks, including a few cancelled shows, the tour ultimately proved to be a financial success. Gilmour's performances, showcasing his virtuosic guitar playing and emotive vocals, were well-received by audiences and critics alike. Nick Mason, Pink Floyd's drummer, even made a guest appearance on the UK leg of the tour, hinting at a possible reconciliation within the band's fractured relationships.

Upon returning from the tour, Gilmour continued to expand his musical horizons. He collaborated with various artists, including folk singer Roy Harper. Their partnership resulted in several co-written songs on Harper's 1980 album "The Unknown Soldier," including

David Gilmour

"Short and Sweet," which had initially been recorded for Gilmour's first solo album. Harper even made a surprise appearance at Gilmour's Hammersmith Odeon gig in 1984, performing "Short and Sweet" alongside him.

Gilmour's collaborative spirit extended to other genres and artists. He lent his guitar talents to Bryan Ferry's 1985 album "Boys and Girls," adding a touch of rock sensibility to Ferry's sophisticated pop sound. He also contributed to the soundtrack of Ridley Scott's fantasy film "Legend," performing the song "Is Your Love Strong Enough" for the US release. The accompanying music video cleverly incorporated footage of Ferry and Gilmour into scenes from the film. In a display of solidarity with the global music community, Gilmour joined Ferry on stage at the Live Aid concert in 1985, a monumental event aimed at raising funds for famine relief in Ethiopia. His participation in this historic event further cemented his status as a respected and influential figure in the music industry.

Gilmour's collaborative streak continued with his contributions to Pete Townshend's 1985 album "White City: A Novel," including the single "Give Blood." He also worked with the enigmatic Grace Jones on her 1985 album "Slave to the Rhythm," adding his distinctive guitar textures to the album's eclectic soundscapes.

David Gilmour

These diverse projects not only showcased Gilmour's versatility as a musician but also highlighted his willingness to step outside his comfort zone and explore new creative avenues. As the 1980s progressed, his solo career continued to flourish, running parallel to his ongoing commitments with Pink Floyd. However, the simmering tensions within the band were far from resolved, and a new chapter was about to unfold that would forever alter the course of their history.

David Gilmour

A NEW ERA OF LEADERSHIP AND CREATIVE VISION

*T*he escalating tensions within Pink Floyd reached a breaking point in 1985 when Roger Waters announced his departure from the band. This decision sparked a bitter legal battle that would reshape the future of Pink Floyd and its legacy. In the lead-up to this pivotal moment, the band members had been pursuing individual projects. Gilmour released his second solo album, "About Face," in 1984, using it as a platform to express his personal views and distance himself from the increasingly strained atmosphere within Pink Floyd. Waters, meanwhile, embarked on a tour to promote his solo album, "The Pros and Cons of Hitch Hiking."

Amidst these solo ventures, the band members met for dinner in 1984 to discuss the future of Pink Floyd. While Gilmour and Mason left the meeting with the impression that the band would continue after Waters completed his tour, Waters interpreted their stance differently. He believed that Gilmour and Mason had accepted Pink Floyd's end. This misunderstanding laid the groundwork for the conflict that would soon erupt. Following the release of "The Pros and Cons of Hitch Hiking," Waters publicly declared that Pink Floyd was finished. He contacted the band's manager, Steve O'Rourke, to discuss settling future royalty payments. However, O'Rourke felt obligated to inform Gilmour and Mason of Waters' intentions, which infuriated Waters and led him to terminate his management contract with O'Rourke.

In December 1985, Waters officially announced his departure from Pink Floyd, sending a letter to EMI and Columbia Records invoking the "Leaving Member" clause in his contract. He believed that the band had become a "spent force creatively" and that continuing without him would be a breach of contract. Waters' actions were driven by a desire to protect his financial interests and prevent the other members from using the Pink Floyd name without his involvement.

Gilmour and Mason, however, were determined to carry on as Pink Floyd. They argued that Waters' departure did not signify the end of the band and that they had the right to continue creating music under the Pink Floyd name. This disagreement led to a protracted legal battle, with Waters seeking to dissolve the Pink Floyd partnership and prevent the remaining members from using the band's name and material. The legal proceedings were contentious and emotionally charged, with both sides making public statements criticising each other. Waters accused Gilmour and Mason of being creatively bankrupt and trying to profit off the Pink Floyd name without his involvement. Gilmour and Mason countered by asserting their right to continue as Pink Floyd and defending their creative contributions to the band.

In the end, the legal battle was settled out of court in December 1987. The terms of the settlement allowed Gilmour and Mason to continue using the Pink Floyd name and performing the band's music. Waters retained the rights to "The Wall" and certain other specific compositions. While the settlement ended the immediate legal conflict, it did not resolve the underlying personal and creative tensions that had led to the split. In retrospect, Waters has expressed regret over the lawsuit, acknowledging that he failed to appreciate the commercial value of the Pink Floyd name independent of the band members. The legal battle, while ultimately resolved, left a lasting scar on the band's legacy, highlighting the complex relationships and creative conflicts that shaped their history.

While Waters' departure was undoubtedly a blow to the band, it also presented a unique opportunity for Gilmour to step into a leadership role. Gilmour, who had always been a crucial creative force within Pink Floyd, now had the freedom to shape the band's sound and direction without the constraints of Waters' often domineering personality. This newfound autonomy allowed him to explore different musical avenues and experiment with new sounds, ultimately leading to a revitalization of Pink Floyd's creative output.

In 1986, Gilmour purchased the Astoria, a houseboat moored on the River Thames near Hampton Court. This unique vessel was transformed into a state-of-the-art recording studio, providing a tranquil and inspiring environment for the band to create new music. The Astoria became a symbol of Pink Floyd's resilience and their determination to continue their musical journey despite the loss of Waters. He began assembling a team of musicians for a new project, initially envisioning it as his third solo album. However, as the creative process unfolded, Gilmour's vision expanded, and he decided to reclaim the Pink Floyd mantle for this new endeavour.

The decision to move forward without Waters was not without its challenges. There were legal hurdles to overcome in reinstating Richard Wright, who had been fired from the band during the recording of "The Wall." Nevertheless, after a meeting in Hampstead, Gilmour and Mason extended an invitation to Wright to rejoin the fold. Gilmour recognized that Wright's presence would not only strengthen their legal position but also enhance the musicality of the project. Wright, eager to return to the band he had helped shape, accepted the offer and was hired as a salaried musician.

Recording sessions commenced on Gilmour's houseboat, the Astoria, moored on the River Thames. This unique setting provided a relaxed and creative atmosphere for the band to explore new ideas and rediscover their musical synergy. Gilmour, who had long felt that Waters' lyrical dominance had overshadowed the music in recent years, sought to restore a balance between the two elements. However, the absence of Waters's creative direction proved to be a challenge. The band struggled to find their footing initially, grappling with the loss of their primary songwriter and conceptual visionary. To address this, Gilmour collaborated with several songwriters, including Eric Stewart and Roger McGough, before ultimately choosing Anthony Moore to contribute lyrics. While Gilmour spearheaded the creative process, Mason and Wright's contributions should not be overlooked. Both musicians had been sidelined during the recording of "The Wall" and were initially out of practice. Gilmour acknowledged that Waters had "destroyed" their confidence, but he remained committed to fostering a collaborative environment where all members could contribute.

In September 1987, "A Momentary Lapse of Reason" was released to the world. The album marked a new chapter for Pink Floyd, showcasing Gilmour's leadership and his vision for the band's future. The cover art, designed by Storm Thorgerson, who had been absent from the band's previous two albums, featured a striking image of hundreds of hospital beds arranged on a beach, symbolising the album's themes of isolation and alienation. While "A Momentary Lapse of Reason" achieved commercial success, reaching number three in both the UK and the US, it was met with mixed reviews. Waters, unsurprisingly, was critical of the album, dismissing it as a "facile forgery" with "poor" songs and "third-rate" lyrics. Gilmour, on the other hand, initially viewed the album as a return to form for the band, a sentiment not shared by Wright, who agreed with Waters' assessment.

The subsequent tour for "A Momentary Lapse of Reason" was a massive undertaking, with the band performing in stadiums across the globe. However, the tour was not without its challenges. Waters attempted to disrupt the tour by contacting promoters and threatening legal action if they used the Pink Floyd name. Gilmour and Mason, determined to carry on, funded the tour themselves, with Mason even using his Ferrari 250 GTO as collateral. Despite Waters' attempts to sabotage the tour, it proved to be a huge success, with Pink Floyd playing to sold-out crowds around the world. The band's live show, featuring elaborate stage sets, stunning visuals, and a carefully curated setlist, captivated audiences and reaffirmed their status as one of the greatest live acts of all time.

In the wake of "A Momentary Lapse of Reason," Pink Floyd retreated from the limelight, engaging in personal projects such as filming and participating in the La Carrera Panamericana race, a gruelling cross-country rally in Mexico. However, the creative spark reignited in 1993 when the band reconvened at Britannia Row Studios to begin work on a new album. The recording process for "The Division Bell" was marked by a collaborative spirit, with Gilmour, Mason, and Wright working together to improvise and generate musical ideas. Within two weeks, they had amassed enough material to start shaping into songs. Bob Ezrin, who had previously co-produced "The Wall," returned to lend his expertise and guidance. The sessions then moved to Gilmour's houseboat, the Astoria, where the band continued to refine their compositions.

Gilmour's influence on "The Division Bell" was undeniable. As the primary songwriter and creative force, he shaped the album's direction, crafting memorable melodies and evocative guitar solos. His songwriting partnership with Polly Samson, who would later become his wife, proved fruitful, with Samson contributing lyrics to several tracks, including the

David Gilmour

In 2009, Gilmour joined his friend and fellow guitar legend Jeff Beck on stage at the Royal Albert Hall for a memorable performance. The two guitarists traded solos and shared the spotlight, showcasing their mutual respect and admiration for each other's talents. Later that year, Gilmour released the online single "Chicago – Change the World," a reworking of the Graham Nash song "Chicago." The single aimed to raise awareness for the case of Gary McKinnon, a British computer hacker facing extradition to the United States. Gilmour's involvement in the campaign highlighted his willingness to use his music to advocate for social justice and individual rights.

This period of Gilmour's career was an indication of his enduring creativity and his ability to reinvent himself as a solo artist while remaining connected to his Pink Floyd roots. His music continued to resonate with fans around the world, and his commitment to social causes further solidified his status as a respected and influential figure in the music industry.

David Gilmour

RECONCILIATION AND FINAL FAREWELLS

*T*he 2010s marked a period of significant events in Gilmour's career, encompassing moments of reconciliation, creative resurgence, and poignant farewells. The decade began with a surprise reunion with Roger Waters, a gesture that offered a glimmer of hope for fans who yearned for a reconciliation between the two Pink Floyd legends.

In July 2010, Gilmour and Waters shared the stage for the first time in over two decades, performing together at a charity event for the Hoping Foundation in Oxfordshire, England. This unexpected collaboration, witnessed by a select audience, seemed to signal a thaw in their long-standing feud. The two were seen laughing and joking together, raising hopes for a more permanent reconciliation. This hope was further fueled in May 2011, when Gilmour joined Waters on stage at the O2 Arena in London during a performance of "The Wall." The two shared a poignant moment during "Comfortably Numb," their iconic duet, as they exchanged smiles and even a brief embrace. Later in the show, Gilmour and Nick Mason joined the rest of the band for a performance of "Outside the Wall," marking a rare and emotional reunion of the Pink Floyd core members.

While the reunion with Waters was a significant event, Gilmour continued to pursue his own creative endeavours. In October 2010, he released an experimental ambient album, "Metallic Spheres," in collaboration with the electronic duo The Orb. This project showcased Gilmour's willingness to explore new musical territories and push the boundaries of his sound.

Despite the legal battles and creative tensions that had plagued Pink Floyd in the 1980s, the band's musical legacy continued to evolve. In a surprising turn of events, Gilmour and Nick Mason decided to revisit a treasure trove of recordings made during the "Division Bell" sessions. These recordings, featuring the late Richard Wright's keyboard contributions, served as the foundation for a new Pink Floyd album.

With a deep sense of respect for Wright's musicality, Gilmour and Mason enlisted the help of session musicians to record new parts and "harness studio technology" to create a fitting tribute to their departed bandmate. The project was not without its challenges, as the band navigated the complexities of creating a cohesive album from archival material. However, their dedication to honouring Wright's legacy fueled their determination. Mason described the resulting album, "The Endless River," as a tribute to Wright's unique musical voice and his integral role in shaping Pink Floyd's sound. He emphasised the importance of recognizing Wright's contributions, stating,

"Listening back to the sessions, it really brought home to me what a special player he was."

Released in 2014, "The Endless River" was met with mixed reviews, with some critics praising its ambient soundscapes and instrumental experimentation, while others found it lacking in lyrical depth and emotional resonance. Nevertheless, the album was a commercial success, becoming the most pre-ordered album on Amazon UK and debuting at number one in several countries. The vinyl edition also broke sales records, becoming the fastest-selling UK vinyl release of 2014 and the fastest-selling since 1997. Gilmour declared that "The Endless River" would be Pink Floyd's final album, stating that they had **"successfully commandeered the best of what there is."** This decision was partly due to Wright's absence, whose unique musical voice was deemed irreplaceable. As Gilmour said, **"It's a shame, but this is the end."**

David Gilmour

Despite the lack of a supporting tour, the release of "The Endless River" marked a poignant conclusion to Pink Floyd's storied career. It served as a tribute to Richard Wright, a final offering from a band that had pushed the boundaries of musical experimentation and left an indelible mark on the history of rock. In the years that followed, Pink Floyd's legacy continued to be celebrated through various archival releases. The "Early Years 1965-1972" box set, released in 2016, compiled a wealth of rare and previously unreleased material from the band's formative years. This was followed in 2019 by "The Later Years," which focused on the band's post-Waters era and included a remixed version of "A Momentary Lapse of Reason" with more contributions from Wright and Mason.

In 2015, David Gilmour embarked on a new solo chapter with the release of "Rattle That Lock," his fourth studio album. This album, a n attestation to Gilmour's enduring creativity and musical evolution, showcased a diverse range of sounds and influences while staying true to his signature guitar work and songwriting prowess. The album's creation was a meticulous process, primarily taking place in Gilmour's personal recording studios, Medina Studio in Hove and the Astoria houseboat studio. These familiar surroundings provided a comfortable and creative environment for Gilmour to explore new musical ideas and experiment with different sounds. Collaborating with longtime engineer Andy Jackson and Damon Iddins, Gilmour crafted a sonic landscape that was both familiar and innovative, drawing inspiration from his past work with Pink Floyd while venturing into new territories.

Phil Manzanera, the album's co-producer, revealed that Gilmour had been working on the material for "Rattle That Lock" for over five years, demonstrating his dedication to crafting a cohesive and well-rounded album. Manzanera also mentioned that one piano piece featured on the album had been recorded 18 years prior in Gilmour's living room, highlighting the long gestation period of some of the musical ideas. The recording process extended beyond Gilmour's personal studios. Orchestra parts were meticulously captured at AIR Studios in London, while the Liberty Choir contributed their powerful vocals in a South London church. The album was then mixed at Astoria and mastered by James Guthrie and Joel Plante at das boot recording in Lake Tahoe, California. This meticulous approach to recording and production ensured that every element of the album was carefully crafted to achieve sonic perfection.

The title track, "Rattle That Lock," emerged from an unlikely source of inspiration. While travelling to visit friends in France, Gilmour recorded the SNCF jingle, a four-note melody used by the French railway company, on his iPhone at Aix-en-Provence station. This simple yet catchy melody sparked Gilmour's imagination, and he incorporated it into the song, transforming it into a driving rock anthem with lyrics written by his wife and frequent collaborator, Polly Samson. The song's lyrics, drawing from themes in John Milton's "Paradise Lost," explore the struggle between good and evil, light and darkness.

Another notable aspect of the album is the contribution of Gilmour's son, Gabriel, who played piano on the track "In Any Tongue." This marked Gabriel's recording debut, adding a personal touch to the album and showcasing the family's shared musical talent. Upon its release in September 2015, "Rattle That Lock" was met with critical acclaim and commercial success. It debuted at number one on the UK charts, making it Gilmour's second solo album to achieve this feat. The album also received positive reviews from critics, who praised its diverse range of musical styles, its introspective lyrics, and Gilmour's signature guitar work.

To amplify the impact of "Rattle That Lock," Gilmour embarked on a multifaceted promotional campaign that encompassed radio airplay, a visually stunning music video, and a global tour. The promotional journey began with the radio premiere of the album's title track on BBC Radio 2's "The Chris Evans Breakfast Show" on July 17th, 2015. This highly anticipated debut immediately made the single available for digital download, generating excitement among fans and critics alike. Gilmour further fueled the anticipation by granting an exclusive interview to U.S. radio DJ Redbeard, where he premiered the entire album on the popular program "In the Studio."

The momentum continued to build as BBC Radio 2 designated "Rattle That Lock" as their "Record of the Week," ensuring widespread exposure and solidifying its place as a standout track. Meanwhile, a visually stunning music video for the song was unveiled on Gilmour's website and social media channels. Created by Trunk Animation under the direction of Alasdair Brotherston and Jock Mooney, the video featured intricate animation and a captivating narrative inspired by John Milton's epic poem "Paradise Lost." This visual representation of the song's themes added another layer of depth and intrigue, further engaging fans and sparking conversations about its meaning.

To bring the music of "Rattle That Lock" to life on a grand scale, Gilmour embarked on a global tour, starting with a special album preview show in Brighton, England, on September 5th, 2015. The tour spanned multiple continents, with performances in Europe, South America, and North America, culminating in a final show in New York City on April 12th, 2016. In addition to the scheduled dates, Gilmour also performed a one-off charity show in Wrocław, Poland, demonstrating his commitment to using his music for a good cause.

The Rattle That Lock Tour was a show of Gilmour's enduring popularity and his ability to captivate audiences with his live performances. The setlist included a mix of songs from his solo albums, Pink Floyd classics, and new material from "Rattle That Lock." Gilmour's virtuosic guitar playing, coupled with the band's tight musicianship and stunning visual production, created an unforgettable experience for fans. A notable highlight of the tour was a special concert at the Roman Theatre of Orange in France. This historic venue, known for its exceptional acoustics and stunning architecture, provided a unique backdrop for Gilmour's music. The concert was also notable for its collaboration with the SNCF, the French railway company, who partnered with Sony Music to celebrate the connection between the song "Rattle That Lock" and their iconic jingle. The tour also included performances at several iconic venues, such as the Royal Albert Hall and KOKO in London, and the Auditorium Theatre in Chicago. These historic locations added a layer of

David Gilmour

significance to the tour, connecting Gilmour's music to
the rich history of rock and roll.

In July 2016, Gilmour returned to the Amphitheatre of
Pompeii, where Pink Floyd had famously filmed their
groundbreaking concert film in 1971. This time, Gilmour
and his band performed two sold-out shows, capturing
the magic and atmosphere of this historic location. The
resulting concert film, "Live at Pompeii," released in
2017, showcased the tour's highlights and offered fans a
unique perspective on Gilmour's live performances. The
film's release was accompanied by a special
one-night-only screening in cinemas worldwide, giving
fans a chance to experience the concert in a unique and
immersive way.

Despite the occasional moments of collaboration and
reconciliation, the relationship between Gilmour and
Waters remained complex and often fraught. The two
continued to clash over issues such as the re-release of
Pink Floyd's back catalogue, the use of the band's name
and logo, and the management of their social media
channels.

Nick Mason, who maintained friendships with Gilmour
and Waters, offered insights into the dynamics of their
relationship. In 2018, he stated that Waters did not
always respect Gilmour's contributions to Pink Floyd,

particularly his guitar playing and singing. Waters, according to Mason, believed songwriting was the most important aspect of the band's creative process and everything else should be secondary.

This fundamental difference in perspective, coupled with their strong personalities and past grievances, made a lasting reconciliation between Gilmour and Waters seem unlikely. However, their occasional collaborations and shared moments on stage offered a glimmer of hope that, despite their differences, they could still find common ground and celebrate the extraordinary musical legacy they had created together.

David Gilmour

PANDEMIC LIVESTREAMS TO A PROTEST SONG

*T*he 2020s brought a wave of unexpected challenges and opportunities for David Gilmour. As the world grappled with the COVID-19 pandemic, he found solace and connection with fans through a series of intimate livestream performances, sharing his music and offering a sense of comfort during uncertain times.

Starting in April 2020, Gilmour invited viewers into his home for a series of online concerts. Joined by his family, he performed a mix of original songs, covers of Syd Barrett's compositions, and Leonard Cohen classics. These livestreams provided a glimpse into Gilmour's personal life, showcasing his musical bond with his family and his unwavering passion for his craft. In July 2020, amidst the pandemic, Gilmour released a new single, "Yes, I Have Ghosts." This poignant song, with lyrics written by Polly Samson and featuring Gilmour's daughter Romany on harp and backing vocals, marked his first solo release since 2015's "Rattle That Lock." The song's ethereal beauty and introspective lyrics resonated with listeners, offering a sense of solace and hope during a challenging time.

David Gilmour

In a remarkable show of solidarity with Ukraine during the tumultuous events of 2022, Pink Floyd, a band that had long been dormant, reemerged with a powerful anthem titled "Hey, Hey, Rise Up!" This unexpected release marked the band's first new music since 2014 and served as a poignant response to the Russian invasion of Ukraine.

The song's genesis can be traced to a viral video posted on Instagram by Andriy Khlyvnyuk, lead singer for Ukrainian band BoomBox. Khlyvnyuk, who had abandoned a US tour to join the Ukrainian military in defence of his homeland, recorded an a cappella version of the Ukrainian folk song "Oh, the Red Viburnum in the Meadow." This stirring rendition, filmed in Kyiv's Sophia Square with the city's iconic Bell Tower of Saint Sophia Cathedral in the background, quickly garnered international attention and became a symbol of Ukrainian resilience in the face of aggression.

Khlyvnyuk's performance deeply moved Gilmour, the legendary guitarist of Pink Floyd,. Having previously collaborated with BoomBox in 2015 for a charity concert supporting the Belarus Free Theatre, Gilmour felt a personal connection to the Ukrainian band and their homeland. Inspired to act, Gilmour reached out to Pink Floyd drummer Nick Mason, proposing a collaboration to create a song in support of Ukraine. The project quickly gained momentum, with Gilmour and Mason enlisting the talents of longtime Pink Floyd bassist Guy Pratt and renowned keyboardist Nitin Sawhney. This marked Sawhney's first collaboration with the band, adding a fresh layer of musicality to their sound. Gala Wright, the daughter of the late Pink Floyd keyboardist Richard Wright, was also present during the recording, offering her support and encouragement.

On March 30th, 2022, the band gathered at Gilmour's home studio and recorded "Hey, Hey, Rise Up!" The song's title, taken from the final line of "Oh, the Red Viburnum in the Meadow," which translates to "Hey, hey, rise up and rejoice," embodied the spirit of Ukrainian resistance and defiance. The song's opening featured a sample from another recording of the Ukrainian anthem by the Veryovka Ukrainian Folk Choir, further emphasising its connection to Ukrainian culture and history. Gilmour, inspired by Khlyvnyuk's impassioned vocals, wrote additional music for the song, including a soaring guitar solo that became a signature element of the track. The resulting composition was a powerful blend of rock and traditional Ukrainian music, a testament to the universality of music as a tool for social commentary and political activism.

David Gilmour

Pink Floyd's decision to release the song under the band's name, despite their previous statements about not reuniting, underscored the urgency and importance of the cause. Gilmour recognized the band's platform and influence and felt compelled to use it to raise awareness about the war in Ukraine and its devastating consequences. The release of "Hey, Hey, Rise Up!" was accompanied by a music video directed by Mat Whitecross. The video featured powerful images of Ukrainian life amidst the backdrop of war, further amplifying the song's message of solidarity and resilience. All proceeds from the song and video were donated to the Ukraine Humanitarian Relief Fund, demonstrating the band's commitment to providing aid and support to those affected by the conflict.

Released on digital platforms and streaming services on April 8th, 2022, "Hey, Hey, Rise Up!" quickly garnered widespread attention and acclaim. It became Pink Floyd's first newly recorded material since the 2014 song "Louder Than Words" and a powerful symbol of their support for Ukraine. The song's emotional resonance and political message resonated with listeners around the world, generating millions of views and streams within days of its release. On July 15th, 2022, a physical version of the single was released on CD and vinyl, further expanding its reach and impact. The physical release also included a newly reworked version of "A Great Day for Freedom," a song from Pink Floyd's 1994 album "The Division Bell." This addition added another layer of depth to the release, highlighting the band's enduring commitment to peace and freedom.

The release of "Hey, Hey, Rise Up!" was met with a mixed response from critics and fans. While many praised the song's emotional power and political message, others questioned the band's decision to release it under the Pink Floyd name without the involvement of Roger Waters or Richard Wright. However, many critics defended the band's decision, arguing that the urgency of the situation and the importance of raising awareness for Ukraine justified their actions. Notably, Roger Waters, who had long been critical of his former bandmates, expressed his disapproval of the song, accusing it of lacking "humanity" and focusing on nationalistic symbolism rather than calling for an end to the war. Waters' controversial stance on the conflict further highlighted the ongoing tensions and disagreements within the Pink Floyd camp.

However, the 2020s also saw a further deterioration in Gilmour's relationship with Roger Waters. In early 2023, Polly Samson publicly criticised Waters on Twitter, accusing him of antisemitism and other negative traits.

David Gilmour

Gilmour echoed his wife's sentiments, saying her words were "demonstrably true." This public exchange highlighted the deep-seated animosity that continued to plague the two former bandmates, casting a shadow over any hope of a lasting reconciliation.

While the future of Pink Floyd remains uncertain, Gilmour's legacy as a musician, songwriter, and activist is secure. He continues to inspire and influence generations of musicians and fans worldwide, and his music remains a testament to the power of human creativity and compassion.

David Gilmour

A NEW CHAPTER

*I*n 2024, David Gilmour embarked on a new chapter in his solo career with the announcement of his fifth studio album, "Luck and Strange," set for release on September 6th. This highly anticipated album marked Gilmour's first collection of new material in nearly a decade and signalled a renewed creative energy. Before the album's release, Gilmour lent his signature guitar sound to a reimagined version of Mark Knopfler's "Going Home: Theme of the Local Hero." This contribution, released in aid of the Teenage Cancer Trust, showcased Gilmour's continued support for charitable causes and his willingness to collaborate with fellow musicians for a good cause.

"Luck and Strange" was recorded over five months in Brighton and London, with producer Charlie Andrew at the helm. Andrew, known for his work with artists like alt-J and Marika Hackman, brought a fresh perspective to Gilmour's music, challenging him to step outside his comfort zone and explore new sonic territories. Gilmour welcomed this challenge, stating that Andrew's **"wonderful lack of knowledge or respect for this past of mine"** pushed him to create something truly unique.

David Gilmour

The album's lyrical content, penned primarily by Polly Samson, delves into themes of mortality, ageing, and the passage of time. Samson's evocative words, combined with Gilmour's soaring melodies and intricate guitar work, create a poignant and introspective listening experience. "Luck and Strange" also features contributions from Gilmour's children. His daughter Romany lends her vocals and harp skills to several tracks, while his son Charlie contributed lyrics to one of the songs. The album also includes previously unreleased keyboard recordings by Richard Wright, a touching tribute to his late bandmate.

The first single from the album, "The Piper's Call," was released on April 25th to critical acclaim. The song's ethereal atmosphere, haunting melody, and evocative lyrics set the tone for the album, hinting at the emotional depth and musical richness that awaited listeners.

The latest single, "Between Two Points," a poignant duet with his daughter Romany Gilmour, offers a tantalising glimpse into the album's multifaceted sonic landscape. The release of this captivating single, featuring Romany's ethereal vocals and delicate harp playing, coincides with the announcement of limited-edition deluxe formats for the album. These exclusive editions, set to become cherished collector's items due to their finite production run, will include bonus tracks and a special hardback book by Thames & Hudson, showcasing intimate photographs taken by Polly Samson during the album's creation.

The album's nine tracks offer a diverse array of sonic landscapes, including a reimagined rendition of The Montgolfier Brothers' 1999 song, "Between Two Points." This evocative piece showcases the unique musical chemistry between David and Romany Gilmour, their voices intertwining with the gentle strains of the harp. Gilmour, a longtime admirer of the song, recognized his daughter's ability to breathe new life into it, resulting in a truly captivating collaboration.

The father-daughter duo's musical connection has been evident in their previous collaborations, such as their live streams as "The Von Trapped Family" during the lockdowns of 2020 and 2021, and their work on the song "Yes, I Have Ghosts," which will be included in the CD & Blu-Ray versions of "Luck and Strange." The effortless harmony between their voices and their shared passion for music shine through in these collaborative endeavours. Mark Tranmer of The Montgolfier Brothers expresses his admiration for Gilmour and Romany's reinterpretation of "Between Two Points," praising the arrangement, production, and the beautiful vocal and harp performances. He finds it incredible that Gilmour and Samson chose to cover their song out of all the possibilities, highlighting the unique connection and artistic appreciation between the two artists.

The accompanying music video for "Between Two Points," filmed in London and Manchester, further showcases the intimate connection between David and Romany. Director Gavin Elder captures the emotional rapport between father and daughter, using handheld cameras to enhance the tension and intimacy of the performance. Romany's vocals and harp playing exude a sense of fragility and vulnerability, while Gilmour's signature guitar work adds a layer of depth and complexity to the song.

To support the album's release, Gilmour announced a limited tour in September 2024. The tour, which will visit four iconic venues – London's Royal Albert Hall, Rome's Circus Maximus, the Hollywood Bowl in Los Angeles, and Madison Square Garden in New York City – promises to be a special event for fans, offering a rare opportunity to experience Gilmour's music in some of the world's most prestigious concert halls. In a move that surprised some fans, Gilmour revealed that he had revamped his touring band, replacing some of the musicians who had accompanied him on previous tours. He explained that he wanted to surround himself with more creative and adventurous players, those who could bring a fresh energy and spontaneity to his live performances.

This decision reflected Gilmour's ongoing dedication to artistic evolution and his desire to push the boundaries of his music. With "Luck and Strange" and his upcoming tour, Gilmour is poised to embark on a new and exciting chapter in his solo career, one that promises to be filled with musical innovation, emotional resonance, and a renewed sense of creative purpose.

THE ALCHEMY OF GILMOUR'S GUITAR

*D*avid Gilmour's distinctive sound, a mesmerising blend of bluesy grit, soaring sustain, and emotive phrasing, has captivated audiences for decades. His guitar playing, a cornerstone of Pink Floyd's sonic sound, is an exemplification of his mastery of the instrument and his ability to evoke a wide range of emotions through music.

Gilmour's musical journey began with a deep immersion in the roots of American music. He cites early blues and folk legends like Pete Seeger and Lead Belly as formative influences, their raw and soulful sounds leaving an indelible mark on his musical sensibilities. As he delved deeper into the world of guitar, he found inspiration in the innovative stylings of British blues rockers like Jeff Beck and Eric Clapton, and the psychedelic explorations of Jimi Hendrix. These diverse influences coalesced into a unique style that would become synonymous with Pink Floyd's sound.

Gilmour's approach to guitar playing is characterised by a deep understanding of melody and a profound emotional connection to his instrument. He eschews flashy displays of technical virtuosity in favour of carefully crafted solos that prioritise feeling and expression. His use of bends, vibrato, and sustain creates a signature sound that is both instantly recognizable and deeply moving. Gilmour acknowledged his limitations as a guitarist, stating, **"I can't play like Eddie Van Halen, I wish I could."** However, he also recognized that his **"fingers make a distinctive sound"** and that his playing is **"instantly recognizable."** This self-awareness and humility, coupled with his strong passion for his craft, have allowed him to continually evolve and refine his style over the decades.

Gilmour's musical influences extend beyond the realm of rock and blues. He cites Joni Mitchell as a major inspiration, particularly her innovative approach to open tunings and her ability to create complex and evocative soundscapes with her guitar. He also draws inspiration from the American primitive guitar styles of John Fahey and the country-inflected blues of Roy Buchanan. These diverse influences have broadened his musical vocabulary and contributed to the eclecticism of his playing.

Beyond the guitar, Gilmour is a multi-instrumentalist, contributing bass, keyboards, and vocals to Pink Floyd's recordings. His bass playing, notably the fretless bass line on "Hey You," demonstrates his versatility and willingness to adapt to different instruments to serve the needs of the song. He has also experimented with other instruments, including the banjo, lap steel guitar, mandolin, harmonica, drums, and saxophone, showcasing his wide-ranging musical interests and curiosity. Gilmour's creative process is often intuitive and improvisational. He prefers to let the music guide him, allowing his emotions and instincts to shape his playing. This approach has led to some of his most iconic and memorable solos, such as the soaring outro of "Comfortably Numb" and the melancholic beauty of "Shine On You Crazy Diamond."

His guitar tone, a crucial component of his sound, is achieved through a combination of vintage and modern equipment. He is known for his use of Fender Stratocaster guitars, Hiwatt amplifiers, and a variety of effects pedals, including the legendary Binson Echorec delay unit. However, Gilmour's tone is ultimately a product of his unique touch and feel, an indication of his intimate connection with his instrument. His guitar playing has inspired countless musicians across genres and generations, and his contributions to Pink Floyd have cemented his place as one of the most iconic and revered figures in rock history. His music continues to resonate with listeners around the world, offering a sonic journey that is both deeply personal and universally relatable.

Gilmour's guitars are not merely tools of his trade, but extensions of his artistic vision, each one imbued with a unique character and history that reflects his diverse musical influences and stylistic evolution. From his early days as a budding guitarist in Cambridge, Gilmour's fascination with the instrument was evident. His first guitar, a white Fender Telecaster gifted to him by his parents for his 21st birthday in 1967, became his constant companion during his formative years with Pink Floyd. This iconic instrument, with its distinctive single-coil pickups and twangy tone, can be heard on early Pink Floyd albums like "A Saucerful of Secrets" and "Ummagumma," adding a bluesy edge to the band's psychedelic soundscapes.

However, it was the acquisition of a black Fender Stratocaster in 1970 that would truly define Gilmour's sonic identity. This guitar, purchased at Manny's Music in New York City after the band's equipment was stolen, became known as the "Black Strat" and quickly became Gilmour's go-to instrument. Over the years, he customised the Black Strat to suit his preferences, swapping out the original rosewood fretboard for a maple one and adding a black pickguard. This iconic guitar can be heard on some of Pink Floyd's most beloved albums, including "The Dark Side of the Moon," "Wish You Were Here," "Animals," and "The Wall." Its versatile tone, capable of producing everything from delicate cleans to searing leads, played a crucial role in shaping the band's sound during their most commercially successful and critically acclaimed period. In 2019, Gilmour auctioned off the Black Strat for a record-breaking $3.9 million, with the proceeds going to charitable causes. This act of generosity not only cemented the guitar's legendary status but also highlighted Gilmour's philanthropic spirit.

Another intriguing instrument in Gilmour's collection is the 0001 Strat, a white Fender Stratocaster with a gold anodized pickguard and gold-plated hardware. This guitar, acquired from his guitar technician Phil Taylor, is believed to be a prototype, possibly predating Fender's commercial release of the Stratocaster. Despite its uncertain origins, the 0001 Strat served as a reliable backup and slide guitar for Gilmour, making appearances on both studio recordings and live performances. In 2019, it was auctioned for $1.815 million, setting a new world auction record for a Stratocaster.

David Gilmour

While Fender Stratocasters hold a special place in Gilmour's heart, he has never been one to shy away from experimenting with other brands and models. During the recording sessions for "The Wall," he utilised a Gibson Les Paul goldtop with P-90 pickups to achieve a thicker, more aggressive tone on tracks like "Another Brick in the Wall, Part 2." He has also been known to play Gretsch Duo-Jet and White Falcon models, and a custom-built "White Penguin" guitar, adding a touch of rockabilly flair to his sonic palette.

Gilmour's versatility extends beyond electric guitars. He is also a skilled acoustic guitarist, having used various models throughout his career, including Gibson Chet Atkins classical and J-200 Celebrity guitars, and Martin D-35 and D12-28 12-string guitars. These acoustic instruments, with their warm and resonant tones, have added a touch of intimacy and folk-inspired charm to Pink Floyd's music, particularly on ballads like "Wish You Were Here" and "High Hopes."

In the early 1970s, Gilmour began experimenting with the pedal steel guitar, a unique instrument known for its expressive, sliding tones. He acquired a Jedson pedal steel from a Seattle pawn shop in 1970, and it's haunting sound can be heard on tracks like "One of These Days" from "Meddle" and "Breathe" and "The Great

David Gilmour

Gig in the Sky" from "The Dark Side of the Moon." Gilmour's innovative use of the pedal steel added a new dimension to Pink Floyd's sonic landscape, creating an ethereal and otherworldly atmosphere that has become synonymous with their music. To capture his unique guitar tone, Gilmour collaborated with EMG, Inc. in 2004 to create the DG20 Signature guitar pickup kit. This active pickup system, based on the configuration of his red Stratocaster used during the "A Momentary Lapse of Reason" and "The Division Bell" tours, allows guitarists to emulate his signature sound, offering a wide range of tonal possibilities, from warm and mellow cleans to aggressive and cutting leads.

His lifelong exploration of different sounds and textures, his willingness to experiment with new technologies, and his strong determination to musical excellence have made him one of the most influential and revered guitarists of all time. His guitars, each with its unique history and character, are a show of his enduring passion for music and his insatiable curiosity about the endless possibilities of sound.

David Gilmour

ADVOCACY AND MUSICAL ACHIEVEMENT

Only his commitment to social justice and humanitarian causes matches Gilmour's passion for music. Throughout his career, he has used his platform and resources to support a wide range of charities and organisations dedicated to improving the lives of others and protecting the planet.

Gilmour's philanthropic endeavours span a variety of issues, reflecting his deep concern for the well-being of both people and the environment. He has been a vocal advocate for organisations such as Oxfam, Greenpeace, Amnesty International, and PETA, lending his voice and financial support to their efforts to combat poverty, protect the environment, and promote human rights.

In the realm of health and well-being, Gilmour has supported the European Union Mental Health and Illness Association, recognizing the importance of mental health care and destigmatizing mental illness. He has also been a patron of the Lung Foundation, raising awareness of lung diseases and supporting research into new treatments.

David Gilmour

Gilmour's love of music has also led him to support Nordoff-Robbins music therapy, a charity that uses music to help people with a range of physical, emotional, and learning disabilities. He believes in the transformative power of music and its ability to heal and connect people on a deep level.

In 1994, he donated £25,000 to the Save the Rhino foundation in exchange for the name suggestion for Pink Floyd's album "The Division Bell." This act of generosity not only helped protect endangered rhinoceroses but also showcased Gilmour's unique approach to fundraising.

Gilmour's commitment to social justice is perhaps most evident in his support for Crisis, a UK-based charity dedicated to ending homelessness. In 2003, he made a substantial donation to Crisis by selling his house in Little Venice, London, for £3.6 million. The proceeds from the sale went towards funding a housing project for the homeless, a cause that Gilmour has been passionate about for many years. He has since been named a vice-president of Crisis, continuing to advocate for the rights and well-being of homeless individuals.

David Gilmour

In 2019, Gilmour made headlines when he auctioned off 120 of his guitars for charity at Christie's in New York. The collection, which included his iconic Black Strat, his #0001 and early 1954 Stratocasters, and his 1955 Les Paul, fetched a staggering $21,490,750. The proceeds from the auction went to ClientEarth, an environmental law charity that uses legal action to protect the planet.

The auction, dubbed "The David Gilmour Guitar Collection," was a landmark event in the world of music memorabilia. The Black Strat alone sold for $3.975 million, making it the most expensive guitar ever sold at auction. Gilmour's decision to part with his beloved instruments for a worthy cause demonstrated his brave commitment to environmentalism and his belief in the power of collective action to create a more sustainable future. His contributions to charitable causes have touched countless lives and inspired others to follow his example. Through his music and his philanthropy, Gilmour has shown that it is possible to achieve both artistic and social success, leaving a lasting legacy that extends far beyond the realm of music.

David Gilmour

Gilmour's contributions to music have not gone unnoticed, as evidenced by the numerous awards and honours he has received throughout his career. These accolades recognize not only his technical prowess as a guitarist and songwriter but also his broader impact on the music industry and his commitment to philanthropic endeavours.

In 2003, Gilmour was appointed Commander of the Order of the British Empire (CBE) in the Queen's Birthday Honors. This prestigious award, bestowed upon him for his "services to music," acknowledged his significant contributions to the cultural landscape of the United Kingdom. The CBE was presented to him at a ceremony at Buckingham Palace on November 7th, 2003, a testament to his enduring legacy and influence.

Gilmour's songwriting talents were further recognized in 2008 when he received the Ivor Novello Lifetime Contribution Award. This prestigious award, presented by the British Academy of Songwriters, Composers, and Authors, celebrated Gilmour's exceptional talent for crafting memorable melodies and evocative lyrics. His body of work, both with Pink Floyd and as a solo artist, stands as a testament to his songwriting prowess and his ability to connect with audiences on a deep emotional level. Later that year, Gilmour was honoured with the Q Award for Outstanding Contribution to Music. This award, presented by the British music magazine Q, recognized his significant impact on the music industry and his enduring popularity as a performer and songwriter. In a poignant gesture, Gilmour dedicated the award to his late Pink Floyd bandmate, Richard Wright, who had passed away just a few weeks earlier.

Gilmour's academic achievements were also acknowledged in 2009 when he received an honorary doctorate from Anglia Ruskin University. This recognition highlighted his contributions to music education and his commitment to inspiring future generations of musicians.

These awards and honours are a proof of David Gilmour's extraordinary talent, his strong dedication to his craft, and his lasting impact on the world of music. They serve as a reminder of his remarkable journey from a young aspiring musician in Cambridge to a global icon, whose music continues to resonate with millions of fans worldwide.

David Gilmour

BEYOND THE STAGE

Gilmour's journey extends far beyond the spotlight and the concert stage, weaving a rich history of personal experiences, deeply held beliefs, and diverse passions. A man of multifaceted interests and a devoted family man, his life offstage is as captivating and inspiring as his musical career. Gilmour's first marriage, to American-born model and artist Virginia "Ginger" Hasenbein in 1975, was a union that brought forth four children: Alice, Clare, Sara, and Matthew. However, the couple's idyllic life in Cambridgeshire was not without its challenges. Their differing views on education, particularly their dissatisfaction with the Waldorf school their children attended, created a rift that ultimately led to their divorce in 1990.

Despite the end of his first marriage, Gilmour's commitment to family remained undeterred. In 1994, he found love again with writer Polly Samson, a woman whose intellect, wit, and creative spirit captivated him. Their wedding ceremony, held in the picturesque surroundings of the countryside, was a testament to their deep connection and shared artistic sensibilities. Storm Thorgerson, Gilmour's longtime friend and the visionary behind Pink Floyd's iconic album artwork, served as best man, symbolising the enduring bonds of friendship and creative collaboration that have shaped Gilmour's life.

Gilmour and Samson's union has been fruitful, both personally and creatively. Samson, an accomplished novelist and lyricist, has become Gilmour's muse and collaborator, co-writing many of the lyrics for his solo albums and contributing to Pink Floyd's "The Division Bell." Their shared passion for music and literature has fostered a deep creative synergy, resulting in some of Gilmour's most poignant and evocative lyrics.

Together, they have built a blended family, raising four children: Charlie, Gilmour's adopted son from Samson's previous relationship with playwright Heathcote Williams, and their biological children, Joe, Gabriel, and Romany. Family has always been a central theme in Gilmour's life and music, and his children have often played a role in his creative endeavours. Charlie's voice can be heard on the telephone at the end of "High Hopes" from "The Division Bell," and Gabriel made his recording debut playing piano on the song "In Any Tongue" from Gilmour's 2015 album "Rattle That Lock."

Gilmour's family life, like any other, has not been without its challenges. In 2011, Charlie was arrested and imprisoned for violent disorder during a student protest in London, an event that deeply affected the family. However, they weathered the storm together, emerging stronger and more united.

Beyond his family life, Gilmour is a man of strong convictions and principles. An avowed atheist, he has spoken openly about his lack of belief in a higher power. His political leanings are firmly on the left, a stance influenced by his parents, who were staunch supporters of the Labour Party and active in social justice movements. Gilmour has inherited their commitment to social equality and has used his platform to advocate for causes he believes in, including environmental protection, animal rights, and humanitarian aid.

Gilmour's interests extend beyond music and politics. A passionate aviator, he holds a pilot's licence and has amassed a collection of historical aircraft. He once owned a company called Intrepid Aviation, dedicated to restoring and preserving vintage aircraft, but later sold it, feeling it had become too commercialised. He still enjoys flying his personal biplane, soaring through the skies and experiencing the freedom and exhilaration of flight. Gilmour's love of history and architecture is evident in his real estate ventures. He has purchased and restored several historic properties, including Hook

David Gilmour

End Manor in Oxfordshire, where parts of Pink Floyd's "The Final Cut" were recorded, and Medina House, a derelict Turkish bathhouse in Brighton and Hove, which he transformed into a stunning family home. He also maintains a residence near the village of Wisborough Green in Sussex, a peaceful retreat where he can escape the demands of his public life. One of Gilmour's most unique properties is Astoria, a houseboat moored on the River Thames near Hampton Court. This floating recording studio, equipped with state-of-the-art technology, has been the birthplace of many of his solo albums and Pink Floyd projects. It is a testament to his creative spirit and his desire to find inspiration in unconventional spaces.

His diverse interests and passions have shaped him into a multifaceted individual, one who is not only an iconic musician but also a thoughtful and engaged citizen of the world. His journey is an attestation to the power of human creativity, compassion, and the enduring pursuit of personal and artistic fulfilment.

David Gilmour

ENDURING INFLUENCE

David Gilmour's impact on the music world extends far beyond his contributions to Pink Floyd. His unique guitar style, characterised by its emotive phrasing, soaring solos, and masterful use of effects, has inspired generations of musicians across genres and continents. He is a revered figure among both classic rock aficionados and younger guitar enthusiasts, bridging the gap between the psychedelic experimentation of the 1960s and the technical virtuosity of later decades.

As MusicRadar aptly put it, Gilmour is **"the missing link between Jimi Hendrix and Eddie Van Halen."** He combines the raw emotional power of Hendrix with the melodic sensibility and technical precision of Van Halen, creating a sound that is both instantly recognizable and deeply influential.

Gilmour's impact is not limited to guitarists. His songwriting, marked by its introspective lyrics and soaring melodies, has resonated with countless music lovers around the world. His ability to craft songs that are both deeply personal and universally relatable has

102

David Gilmour

earned him a place among the most respected and admired songwriters of his generation. Gilmour's recognition as a musical icon is evident in the numerous accolades and awards he has received throughout his career. In 1996, he was inducted into the Rock and Roll Hall of Fame as a member of Pink Floyd, a testament to the band's enduring legacy and their impact on popular culture. He has also been consistently ranked among the greatest guitarists of all time by prestigious publications such as Rolling Stone and The Daily Telegraph.

In 2007, Guitar World readers voted Gilmour's solos on "Comfortably Numb," "Time," and "Money" among the top 100 greatest guitar solos of all time, further solidifying his reputation as a master of his craft. In 2011, Rolling Stone named him the 14th greatest guitarist of all time, placing him alongside such legends as Jimi Hendrix, Eric Clapton, Jimmy Page, and Keith Richards.

Gilmour's influence is not confined to the realm of professional musicians. His music has inspired countless aspiring guitarists to pick up the instrument and explore their own creativity. His solos, with their melodic phrasing and emotional depth, have become a benchmark for aspiring players, encouraging them to strive for a similar level of artistry and expression.

David Gilmour

Several notable musicians have cited Gilmour as a major influence on their own playing. Steve Rothery, guitarist of progressive rock band Marillion, credits Gilmour as one of his three main influences, alongside Jimi Hendrix and Steve Hackett. John Mitchell, the guitarist of It Bites and Arena, has also acknowledged Gilmour's impact on his playing, particularly his use of melody and tone.

In 2013, Gary Kemp, the guitarist and songwriter of Spandau Ballet, and a member of Nick Mason's Saucerful of Secrets, went so far as to declare Gilmour's work on "The Dark Side of the Moon" as the pinnacle of guitar playing in recent history. This sentiment, echoed by many fans and critics alike, highlights the enduring power and influence of Gilmour's music.

David Gilmour's legacy is one of undying artistic integrity, a relentless pursuit of musical excellence, and a profound impact on the lives of countless musicians and music lovers. His music continues to inspire, challenge, and captivate, ensuring that his name will forever be etched in the pantheon of rock and roll greats.

Made in the USA
Middletown, DE
11 September 2024

60797542R00064